MY
PRA

MW00719649

Written by Robert Drapeau

Illustrations: Jepree V. Manalaysay

TABLE OF CONTENTS

Library of Congress Control Number: 2011910782
ISBN 978-1-936020-26-3

The Story of the Rosary

The Rosary is a special kind of prayer called *contemplative prayer*. When we pray the Rosary, we think about events from the lives of Jesus and Mary. We call these events "mysteries," because they teach us something about the love of God. As we pray the Rosary, we open up our hearts to God. We also learn new things about God.

A long, long time ago, Catholic Christians prayed the 150 Psalms every day. They kept track with a pebble—one for each Psalm. As time passed, people replaced the Psalms with the prayers of the Our Father, the Hail Mary, and the Gloria. They also replaced the pebbles with a string of beads from which hung a crucifix.

This book will help you pray and meditate on the mysteries of the Rosary. You will find something to think about for each of the mysteries. You will see how much God loves you and how special Our Lady is.

Each prayer of the Rosary is like a rose we offer to Our Mother Mary. When we pray, our hearts—like our fingers on the beads—draw us closer to Jesus.

The Prayers of the Rosary

Our Father

Our Father, Who art in heaven,
hallowed be Thy name.
Thy kingdom come, Thy will be done,
on earth as it is in heaven.

Give us this day our daily bread;
and forgive us our trespasses,
as we forgive those who trespass against us;
and lead us not into temptation,
but deliver us from evil. Amen.

Hail Mary

Hail Mary, full of grace,
the Lord is with thee.
Blessed art thou among women,
and blessed is the fruit
of thy womb, Jesus.

Holy Mary, Mother of God,
pray for us sinners,
now and at the hour of our death. Amen.

Glory Be

Glory be to the Father, and to the Son,
and to the Holy Spirit;
as it was in the beginning,
is now, and ever shall be,
world without end. Amen.

Fatima Prayer

O my Jesus, forgive us our sins;
save us from the fires of hell.
Lead all souls to Heaven,
especially those most in need of Your mercy.

Hail, Holy Queen

Hail, Holy Queen, Mother of Mercy,
Our life, our sweetness, and our hope!
To thee do we cry, poor banished
children of Eve; to thee do we send
up our sighs, mourning and weeping
in this valley of tears. Turn then,
most gracious advocate, thine eyes
of mercy towards us; and after this
our exile, show unto us the blessed
fruit of thy womb, Jesus.
O clement, O loving, O sweet Virgin Mary.

The Apostles' Creed

I believe in God, the Father almighty,
Creator of heaven and earth,
and in Jesus Christ, his only Son, our Lord,
who was conceived by the Holy Spirit,
born of the Virgin Mary,
suffered under Pontius Pilate,
was crucified, died, and was buried.

He descended into hell;
on the third day
he rose again from the dead;
he ascended into heaven,
and is seated at the right hand
of God the Father almighty;
from there he will come to judge
the living and the dead.

I believe in the Holy Spirit,
the holy catholic Church,
the communion of saints,
the forgiveness of sins,
the resurrection of the body,
and life everlasting. Amen.

The Mysteries of the Rosary

There are 20 mysteries of the Rosary. These mysteries are based on scenes from the lives of Jesus and Mary.

The five **Joyful Mysteries** are events in the life of Mary and the early life of Jesus. We pray the Joyful Mysteries of the Rosary on Mondays and Saturdays.

The five **Luminous Mysteries** are drawn from the public ministry of Jesus. Blessed John Paul II introduced these mysteries of the Rosary. We pray them on Thursdays.

The five **Sorrowful Mysteries** remind us of the Passion and Death of Jesus. We pray the Sorrowful Mysteries on Tuesdays and Fridays.

The five **Glorious Mysteries** of the Rosary celebrate the victory of Jesus over sin and death. They also celebrate Our Blessed Mother Mary and her part in God's plan. We pray these mysteries on Wednesdays and Sundays.

THE JOYFUL MYSTERIES

When we pray the Joyful Mysteries of the Rosary, we think of how joyful Mary must have been. God chose Mary from all women to be the Mother of His Son, Jesus. No other person has ever been so blessed.

The Joyful Mysteries also remind us of the many joys we experience in our family life, such as the happiness and excitement that a new mother feels with her baby. Our parents feel happy when they meet people who love and care about their children. They also feel relief when they find a child whom they thought was lost.

We call Mary the Cause of our Joy because, through her, our world received the most wonderful gift ever: Jesus, Our Redeemer! O come, let us adore Him.

The First Joyful Mystery:
The Annunciation

In Nazareth, a small village of Israel, there lived a lovely young lady named Mary. Mary was pure and filled with grace from the very first moment of her life. She was engaged to be married to a young carpenter named Joseph. Joseph was a descendant of King David.

One day, the archangel Gabriel appeared to Mary from heaven. He said, "Do not be afraid, Mary, for you have found favor with God. Behold, you will give birth to a son, and you shall call him Jesus. He will be great, and he will be called the Son of the Most High God." Mary said, "Let it be done unto me according to your word."

The Second Joyful Mystery:
The Visitation

The angel Gabriel gave Mary more good news: her beloved cousin Elizabeth was going to have a baby in her old age! This made Mary very happy. Mary wanted to help her cousin. She hurried to the hill country where Elizabeth and her husband Zechariah lived.

As Mary drew near to their house, she called out a greeting. When Elizabeth heard Mary's voice, the baby inside her jumped for joy! Elizabeth felt so special that the mother of God would visit her. "Blessed are you among women and blessed is the fruit of your womb!" she exclaimed. In response, Mary joyfully sang, "My soul proclaims the greatness of the Lord, and my spirit rejoices in God my savior."

The Third Joyful Mystery:
The Nativity

In those days, the Roman Emperor, Caesar Augustus, decreed that a census should be taken and that all the people should return to their hometowns to be counted. Because Joseph was a descendant of David, he and Mary journeyed to Bethlehem, the city of David.

When the time came for Mary to have her baby, they had no place to stay. Mary was not afraid. She trusted God and Joseph. After searching everywhere, Joseph finally found a stable in Bethlehem. He lovingly led Our Lady inside, and there among the lowly animals, Jesus was born. He was the world's first Christmas present. Outside, angels sang, "Glory to God in the highest! Peace to His people on earth!"

The Fourth Joyful Mystery:
The Presentation in the Temple

When the time came for their purification according to the Law of Moses, Mary and Joseph went to Jerusalem to offer a sacrifice and to present Jesus in the temple. There they met Simeon, a righteous man. God had promised Simeon that he would not die until he had seen the Messiah. Simeon took Jesus in his arms and prayed, "Now, Master, You may let Your servant go in peace, according to Your word, for my eyes have seen Your salvation."

Simeon then told Mary that Jesus was destined to be the fall and rise of many in Israel. He said, "A sword will pierce your own soul as well, so that the thoughts of many hearts may be revealed." Mary wondered what Simeon meant.

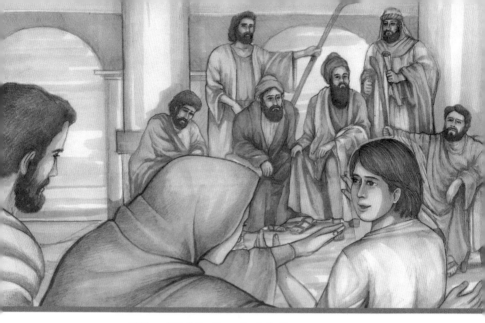

The Fifth Joyful Mystery:
The Finding of Jesus in the Temple

Jesus grew in wisdom and strength. Every year, Joseph and Mary traveled with him to Jerusalem to celebrate the Passover. When Jesus was 12, they went up to Jerusalem as usual, but Jesus stayed behind without telling his parents.

As they journeyed home, Mary and Joseph looked for Jesus among their friends and family. When they realized Jesus was not with them, Mary and Joseph returned to Jerusalem. They found Jesus in the temple speaking to the elders, amazing all who heard him. Mary asked, "Son, why have you done this to us?" Jesus answered, "Did you not know that I must be about my Father's business?" Jesus returned home and was obedient to his parents. Mary kept his words in her heart.

THE LUMINOUS MYSTERIES

In the Luminous Mysteries, we learn things about Jesus, who was both God and man. Before Jesus came into the world, no one could see God. After Jesus came, people could see with their own eyes how much God loved them. By praying these mysteries, we can also come to see how much God wants to give Himself to us.

We see Jesus with other people, doing what they do, joining them in their happy celebrations. We see Jesus telling sinners to be good, so that all of God's children can be happy with Him forever. Finally, we see at the Last Supper how Jesus gives Himself—Body, Blood, Soul, and Divinity—to the Apostles and to all of us. He gives us Himself so that when we remember Him, especially at Holy Mass, He is truly present with us.

The First Luminous Mystery:
The Baptism in the Jordan

Jesus' cousin John, the son of Elizabeth and Zechariah, grew up and became a prophet. He baptized people in the Jordan River, and told them to repent and make straight the way of the Lord. When Jesus came to the Jordan to be baptized, John saw him and exclaimed: "Behold the Lamb of God!"

Jesus wanted John to baptize him, but John felt unworthy. Jesus insisted, so John baptized him. Afterwards, a voice from heaven said, "This is My beloved Son in whom I am well pleased." The Holy Spirit came upon Jesus like a dove and drove him into the wilderness. Jesus fasted and prayed for forty days. Then he was ready to begin his work.

The Second Luminous Mystery:
The Wedding at Cana

Mary, Jesus, and the disciples were invited to a wedding in the village of Cana in Galilee. During the feast, the newlyweds ran out of wine. Mary, who always takes care of her loved ones, told Jesus, "They have no wine." To the servers she said, "Do whatever he tells you."

At the feast, there were six stone jars filled with water for washing. Jesus told the servers to fill them to the brim and to take a sample to the wine steward. The steward was amazed at what he tasted! It was not water anymore. It had become wine—the best he had ever drunk. This was Jesus' first miracle, and his disciples began to believe in him.

The Third Luminous Mystery:
The Proclamation of the Kingdom

After John the Baptist was arrested by King Herod, Jesus began preaching in Galilee. He said, "The kingdom of God is at hand. Repent and believe in the Gospel!" The Gospel is Good News. God loves us so much that He sent his only Son, Jesus, into the world. Whoever believes in Jesus will live forever. Jesus wants to be the King of our hearts.

For three years Jesus traveled throughout Israel showing God's love in many ways. Jesus had come to show people the way to God—He is the Way! He came to tell them the truth about God—He is the Truth! He came to give them the Life of God—and Jesus is Himself the Life we need!

The Fourth Luminous Mystery: The Transfiguration

One day, Jesus took Peter, James, and John up onto a high mountain to pray with him. While Jesus was praying, he was transfigured. His face started to shine like the sun and his clothes became dazzling white. Then, two men—Moses and Elijah—appeared next to Jesus, also in brilliant white. They spoke about Jesus' upcoming Passion and Death.

While Moses and Elijah were speaking, the three Apostles, who had all fallen asleep, awoke. Peter offered to put up three tents for Jesus and his visitors, but then, a voice spoke from a cloud. "This is my beloved Son," God said. "Listen to Him." Moses and Elijah disappeared, and Jesus was again alone with his disciples.

The Fifth Luminous Mystery:
The Gift of the Eucharist

On the night before he died, Jesus and his Apostles shared their last supper together. Jesus told them, "I have eagerly desired to eat this Passover with you before I suffer." Jesus, the Lamb of God, knew that he would be sacrificed the next day for the sins of the world. However, on the night before he died, Jesus wanted to give his friends a very special present: his Presence.

At the Last Supper, Jesus celebrated the first Mass. He took bread, blessed it, and said, "Take and eat, all of you. This is My Body." Then, taking the wine, he said, "This cup is the new covenant in My Blood, shed for you." He told them, "Do this in remembrance of me."

THE SORROWFUL MYSTERIES

When we pray the Sorrowful Mysteries, we see how much Jesus loves us. In the Garden of Eden, Adam and Eve disobeyed God and lost His friendship. In the Garden of Gethsemane Jesus prayed to his Father, "Let it be, not as I will, but as You will." It is his loving obedience that restores our friendship with God.

The Sorrowful Mysteries also show us how hurtful our sins are. The people whom Jesus came to save rejected him. They beat him and made fun of him. They shouted, "Crucify him! Crucify him!" In spite of all this, Jesus prayed, "Father, forgive them, for they know not what they do." Jesus loves us so very much!

The First Sorrowful Mystery:
The Agony in the Garden

After the Last Supper, Jesus and his Apostles went to the Garden of Gethsemane to pray. He took Peter, James, and John, aside and told them, "My soul is sorrowful unto death. Remain here and keep watch with me." Then, in prayer, Jesus begged his Father, "If it is possible, let this suffering pass from me; yet not as I will, but as You will."

When Jesus returned, he found his disciples asleep. He asked them, "Could you not watch one hour with me?" Just then, Judas, one of the disciples, appeared. He brought soldiers with him to arrest Jesus and take him away. With a kiss, Judas betrayed his best friend.

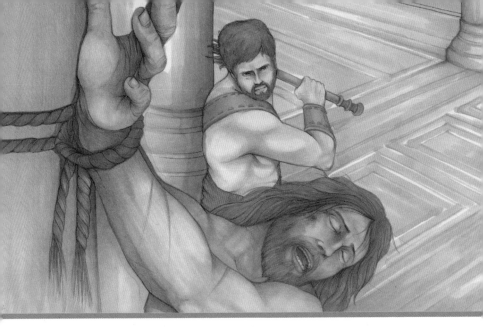

The Second Sorrowful Mystery:
The Scourging at the Pillar

The soldiers took Jesus to the temple to stand trial before the High Priest. The Jewish leaders treated him unfairly and repeatedly hurt him. They wanted him to be killed for the crimes they said he committed. However, only Pontius Pilate, the Roman governor, was allowed to put someone to death.

The Jewish leaders brought Jesus to Pilate for questioning. Pilate found no fault in him, but to satisfy the leaders, he ordered that Jesus be tied to a post and whipped. Jesus was covered with deep wounds all over his body. This fulfilled what the prophet Isaiah had prophesied: "By his stripes we were healed."

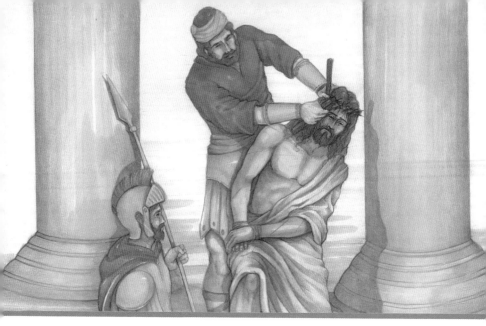

The Third Sorrowful Mystery: The Crowning with Thorns

The Jewish leaders accused Jesus of claiming to be a king. They turned the people against Jesus. Pilate asked Jesus if he was a king. Jesus answered, "You have said so."

The soldiers placed a scarlet robe on Jesus to mock him. They made a crown of thorns for his head and knelt before him. They said, "Hail, King of the Jews!" They hit Jesus over the head, which hurt him very much.

Then they brought Jesus back to Pontius Pilate. Pilate said to the crowd, "Behold the man!" He thought that they might change their minds and let Jesus live. But the people cried out, "Crucify him!"

The Fourth Sorrowful Mystery:
The Carrying of the Cross

The soldiers made Jesus carry his cross up Mount Calvary, where he would be crucified. Many years before that time, Abraham's son Isaac had also carried the wood upon which he would be sacrificed to the top of a mountain. God spared Abraham's son, but, out of love for us, He did not spare His own dear son, Jesus.

Jesus was beaten so badly that he could barely walk. His cross was so heavy and he was so weak! The soldiers were afraid that Jesus would die on the way. They forced Simon of Cyrene to carry the cross behind Jesus. Jesus had told everyone, "If anyone wants to be my disciple, let him take up his cross and follow me."

The Fifth Sorrowful Mystery:
The Crucifixion

Mother Mary stood at the foot of the cross. When she saw the soldiers pierce Jesus' hands and feet, she remembered the words of Simeon. When Jesus was a baby, Simeon had spoken of a sword that would pierce her soul. Now it did.

Mary heard Jesus pray, "Father, forgive them for they know not what they do." From the cross, Jesus gave Mary to his beloved apostle, John. Then Jesus gave John to his mother Mary. After he died, some disciples took the broken body of Jesus from the cross and placed him in Mary's arms. Mary felt the same tender love in her heart that she had felt when Jesus was a baby. Like God the Father, Mary gave her only son so that the world might live.

THE GLORIOUS MYSTERIES

When we pray the Glorious Mysteries, we praise God for the great victory Jesus has won. The Resurrection proves that sin and death no longer rule over us. Jesus has conquered death! Heaven is open to all people!

Jesus sends the Holy Spirit to guide and comfort us. Through the Holy Spirit, the Church continues the work of Jesus. The Church invites everyone to receive Jesus in their hearts and to obey Him. When Jesus lives in our hearts we are living in the Kingdom of God. Our Blessed Mother Mary helps us and gives us hope. We pray that someday all of God's children will share in the glory of Christ's Resurrection just as Mary already does.

The First Glorious Mystery:
The Resurrection

Jesus died and was buried on Good Friday. The next day, the chief priests and the Pharisees asked Pilate to seal the tomb of Jesus and to post a guard. They were worried that some of His followers might steal His body to make it look like He rose from the dead. Pilate allowed them to seal the tomb and he sent soldiers to guard it.

On Sunday morning, some women went to the tomb to anoint the body of Jesus. Suddenly, an earthquake shook the ground and an angel rolled away the stone. Jesus arose from the dead! The guards ran away in fear. The angel told the women, "He is not here. He has risen as He said. Go, tell His disciples!"

The Second Glorious Mystery:
The Ascension

After the Resurrection, Jesus appeared to His disciples. First, He spoke to the women who had come to His tomb. Then He walked to the village of Emmaus with two other disciples. They did not recognize Him. Jesus revealed Himself to them—first in the Scriptures and then in the breaking of the bread.

Jesus appeared in the upper room to His Apostles. He gave them the Holy Spirit and the power to forgive sins. At the end of forty days, Jesus blessed His Apostles. He sent them out into the world to preach the Gospel and baptize in the name of the Father, the Son, and the Holy Spirit. Then Jesus went back up into heaven on a cloud. Heaven was finally open to all people! Jesus had won!

The Third Glorious Mystery:
The Descent of the Holy Spirit

Before He returned to heaven, Jesus promised His apostles that the Holy Spirit would come upon them in power. Mary and the Apostles prayed and waited together in the upper room. Suddenly, on the feast of Pentecost, a noise like a rushing mighty wind came from heaven, filling the whole house. The Holy Spirit came down in tongues as of fire and rested on everyone in the room.

The Holy Spirit filled Mary and the disciples with His gifts, to strengthen and enlighten them. The Apostles were finally ready to spread the Gospel. The Holy Spirit leads all believers, and all of us, to truth through the Church. Does the Church have a birthday? Yes! It is Pentecost Sunday!

The Fourth Glorious Mystery:
The Assumption

When her earthly life was over, the Virgin Mary was taken up body and soul into heaven. She is the first person to share fully in the glory of her Son's Resurrection. We believe that one day, our bodies and souls will also be reunited in heaven, like Mary's body and soul.

After Jesus died, arose, and returned to heaven, the apostle John cared for Mary for many years. In turn, Mother Mary comforted and consoled John and the other Apostles. Because Jesus loves the whole Church, Mary is also the Mother of the whole Church. From heaven, Mary continues to comfort and console all of her children.

The Fifth Glorious Mystery:
The Crowning of Our Lady as Queen of Heaven

In all of creation, there is no creature greater than the Virgin Mary, for only she was blessed to be the Mother of God. From Mary, Jesus received His humanity—His body and His blood. How alike they must have been!

On earth, Jesus honored His mother by listening to her and caring for her. In heaven, He honors her in a special way: He crowns her as Queen of heaven and earth, Queen of all the angels and saints! Jesus is the Lord of lords and the King of kings. Mother Mary shared fully in His work of redemption on earth. It is right, then, that she should share also in His glory in heaven. With great joy, the angels and saints proclaim, "Hail Holy Queen!"

Holding Mary's Hand

A little boy named Joey had to cross a bridge all by himself on his way to school each day. Joey would always cross the bridge very slowly, because he was afraid that he might fall. Therefore, Joey was always late for school.

One day, Joey came to school bright and early. His teacher said, "Joey, did you find another way to school?" "No," Joey said, "I had to cross the bridge the same as always. But today, my Mother walked with me!"

Mary is your Mother in heaven. She loves you! When you pray the Rosary, you hold Mary's hand. You walk with her to Jesus. When we are with Jesus and Mary, we are home!

Pray the Rosary with Mother Mary every day!